Wholesome Dystopia Vol 1.

Madeleine Kelly

Wholesome Dystopia Vol 1. © 2023
Madeleine Kelly

All rights reserved.

Madeleine Kelly asserts the moral right to be identified as author of this work.

Presentation by *BookLeaf Publishing*

Web: www.bookleafpub.com

E-mail: info@bookleafpub.com

ISBN: 9789357212946

First edition 2023

ACKNOWLEDGEMENT

If you are reading this, I am proud of you.

Listening

The Universe speaks
More clearly to those she
Knows will be listening.

Sonnet #1

I know not of love, but I know for thee
My feelings seem to grow like fervid weed.
For as long as my heart bleeds, when need be
I will feed thee, as water does the seed
To whet its hunger deep for sun and play.
As I need thee, like sunrise needs sunset
To behold the beauty of Summer's day.
I see thee, as when the moon and night met
So in brightness and brilliance, they basked.
And I remember when the waves bet moon
They would dance in whichever way she asked
If stars could watch sand dunes.
And I swear, when the stars were asked to
choose,
They said, the better to be nearer, you.

The Girl in the Glass

I fell in love at first sight this morning. It was no extraordinary morning, at first. My mood was neutral, and so was the sky. No enchanting songbirds serenaded me. No warmth from the morning rays basked me in comforting serenity. Even the fresh summer breeze was acting lackluster.

But then, I saw her. Standing there, going about her business. Dressed in a tattered, woven sweater, so oversized it might have been a blanket. Her hair was disheveled, with wavy wisps billowing around her head, grasped haphazardly by a wherewithal clip.

Tangled copper locks framed a cherubic face, and full rosy cheeks were accentuated by a pair of dimples that giggled when she noticed my gaze. Her nose fell somewhere between delicate and well-defined, rounded yet pronounced with a ridge that told me stories of childhood roughhousing, freewheeling and whimsical carelessness.

Her eyes shone brightly despite their darker hue, with obsidian pupils surrounding Tiger's Eye irises, checkered with onyx, pyrite and carnelian. Her skin was fair, except for all the bronzed edges of her body that told of afternoon walks along the river and clandestine tropical getaways.

It's a surreal sense of safety to know a face you've never seen. The idiosyncrasies of a soul can not be disguised by a new, still unfamiliar mask.

And yet, I allowed myself to indulge in a rush of delight pondering all the past lives we shared together, sipping dark roast from my mug, as she did the same.

I smiled wide at her mischievous grin, and whispered, "I love you," through the glass. Tears sprouted like April tulips from the beds of both our eyelashes.

Revolt

To love yourself
Is a revolutionary
Political act.

Spirit Cybernetics

Your brain and body is a machine designed for success by divine powers, instilled with mechanisms which enable you to learn and grow with every thought and action. Ever since you first came Earthside, you've been grasping for objects never yet beheld by you, breathing with lungs that never before held air, and uttering sounds that reflect a language you had only ever heard from a muffled distance. The truth is, your nervous system cannot tell the difference between your imagination and reality. It reacts according to what you believe to be true. Ordinary people have undergone surgery after being hypnotized into believing they can not feel pain. Their bodies know that pain is simply a matter of perception. In the same way, you can hypnotize yourself into believing that you are invincible. Repeat these words to yourself every day, until you believe them: I am smart. I am strong. I am successful. I am worthy of happiness and I'm grateful for the miracle that is my life. Mesmerize yourself with your own mantras, and one day you will wake up re-programmed as the person you always wanted to be. Remember, you are a machine with mechanisms designed to succeed. This is your manual.

Dopamine

The first joy we find
Catching shadows in the dawn
Will be chased by stars.

Power

Love is the power
To peer into a mirror
And see your true self.

Love is the power
To build a home with no walls
And still know safety.

Love is the power
To cast light on flawed weakness
And see strength's shadow.

Love is the power
To befriend our enemies,
Both inside and out.

Love is the power
To know it's never killed,
Only neglected.

Love is the power
To inspire peace and war,
While fighting both sides.

Love is the power
To let down our arms at last
And know true freedom.

Boundaries

Love is many things.
Above all, boundless freedom.
So, no things at all.

Circles

The sun will set, and rise on the other side.
A flower blooms, becomes soil, feeds the next
born.
The wave reaches shore, and melts back into
tide.
A cloud rains down, and resurrects in the morn.
Summer becomes winter, then spring, then the
Fall.
Roots will keep drinking, even when they've
been torn.
White is made of rainbows, yet holds none at all.
People stand still although their world is
spinning.
There is no darkness, just light we can't recall.
When it seems we are losing, we are winning.
There are no endings, only new beginnings.

Bookends

13

There can be no pleasure without pain. And without pain, there is no pleasure. They work together as bookends on the spectrum of human experience. But in the endless purgatory of unrequited love, there is neither pain nor pleasure. Only infinite, unfulfilled, hopeless potential.

Purgatory

What happens when I wake up?
What happens when I fall
Away from the stars
Who blazed the path before me?
What happens when I soar
So high that by all of Nature's laws
I must come plummeting
D
O
W
N
?
The pull of the moon and a lifetime of wishes
Can only hold so much.
How will I know how far I have left to fly
Before I find that
Perilous state, where the wind can no longer
Carry my weight?
The farther away that I stray from my
comfortable rock,
The more I strain against the bounds of its
knowable orbit.
I thought it would be darker here.
This liminal space between home
And hope.

But there is brightness here.
This purgatory I heard them call
Potential.
So much light it blinds me, yet I try my best
To will my eyes cast a wider net.
I can not miss an errant beam. There is no way
to tell
From which way the light
Streams.
They envelop my vision, pouring into my senses
Until I am drenched in its daze,
Swimming in an inchoate swamp.
Am I floating or am I
S i n k
i n g
?
Perhaps I am merely
Standing still. So still,
I perceive the rotations
Of my rock as
V E L O C I T Y .
Perhaps the darkness is in fact
So black
My mind can not fathom it's
Depth.
Perhaps the beams are just a mirage,
Reflecting off the imposter
That lives
In the mirror

Of my reality.
I know,
In a moment I'll open my eyes
To see this was all a dream,
And all there will be left
To wonder is how
A nothingness
Like me can
sleep?

Every story has its chapter...

17

I was always judged
By just my cover, so now
I'm an open book.

Vacancy for Hope

I bought my dream home
With a stranger named Soulmate,
But it was haunted.

We lived with our ghosts
And broke bread with our demons,
Like they were family.

Our home became Hell.
A bed and breakfast for spite,
Evicting all trust.

We put up a sign
That said: "VACANCY FOR HOPE!"
But no angels knocked.

So, bankrupt of love,
We replaced hope with "FOR SALE!"
And packed our baggage.

Our property boasts
Picturesque views of red flags,
Felled pine trees and sunsets.

Fresh renovations
Like stainless steel confessions
And tripled-paned shame.

Rooms painted in hues
Of changed games and broken rules
My fears, hanging framed.

Backyard garden beds
Sewn with buried needs, boundaries,
And burnt memories.

Neighbours with pitchforks
Scour yard sales for lessons.
Homelessness, or Hope?

Here, devils hide horns
Behind porch light halos and
White picket fences.

Cups

When you're so used to
Overflowing, being
Whole still feels shallow.

Safe House

Where do you go when your safe house is
infested,
overrun by slithering egos, venomous lies and
false idols
eating away at the
floorboards?
What do you do when every room
was built on a faulty
foundation,
upsetting the graves of every wraith to walk the
white picketed path
before you?
When do you learn to give up all hope of
restoring what can bever be restored
because it was never there
to begin with?
How do you sleep with the suffering dawn
reaching around bars on your
window?
Why is hiding
under the bed lying
amongst dust bunnies and monsters
in your own makeshift coffin
more comforting that the illumination of a
nightlight?

Saved

It is clear to me:
We will be saved by the Arts,
Teaching us Freedom.

Survival

I have known truth to be a liar.
I have seen an Angel sin.
I have watched water burn through fire.
I have made the devil grin.

I have shown mercy to the face of guilt.
I have dressed innocence in crime.
I have crossed bridges yet to be built.
I have aged backwards in time.

I have marched up to that pearly gate.
I have been saved by demon spawn.
I have learned to Love from teacher Hate.
I have withered in the light of dawn.

I have thrived in an era of drought.
I have conspired against heart and mind.
I have felt safe with pain and faith in doubt.
I have birthed kin not of my kind.

I have sailed the world in a sinking ship.
I have raised unborn babies from the dead.
I have been on journeys that missed the trip.
I have slept with enemies in a king-sized bed.

Enough

Someday, you will meet
Someone who sees your Too Much,
And asks you for more.

The Tiger

I feel like I must take up space.
I owe it to my ancestors.
I owe it to my mother.

I owe it to myself.

I owe it to every woman that has ever been told
she is too much.

But sometimes, I just want to sit.
Tinkering with my energy
Carefully, like a missile
S i m m e r i n g.

Do not mistake my silence for obedience.
Do not take my stillness as inaction.
Do not believe my peace reveals weakness.

Like a Tiger waiting in the reeds,
The more lethal I become.

Now, run.

Sacrifice

Thwack.

My axe connects to ancient flesh, blade sticky with sweet blood.

Thwack.

"I'm sorry," I whisper, heart breaking with the bark.

Thwack.

"I had no choice," I sob, resolve hardening my jaw.
Thwack.

"You did this," I hiss, voice quivering like the string of a bow after its first fatal blow.

Thwack.

Shock pummels my bones with the force of an ocean eroding boulders into stones.

Thwack.

One last slash and it hemorrhages, hitting
sacrificial ground with the sound of a blackhole
birthing oblivion.

My match meets pyre and gasoline, 'till the only
trace left of you is ashes.

The Doors

In case you were wondering,
There is no heaven or hell.
Just a room full of doors
And their adjacent doorbells.

Let me paint you a picture,
Since you asked so politely.
But I can't tell you too much.
Life's a mystery, quite rightly.

Should you ever wake up alone
In a ballroom painted maroon,
Then your soul has left Earth
And returned home to the moon.

When I first saw those walls,
I stood up, shocked and confused.
When I finally called out for help,
A cloaked figure appeared, bemused.

"Salutations, my friend!"
The hooded creature said.
"What happened?" I asked.
"Well, my dear, you are dead."

"Oh shit." I exclaimed, finally coming to.
"If this isn't a joke, it's pretty big news.
I'm a tad disappointed, to tell you the truth.
I thought the afterlife would have better views."

"Trust me, there is more for you to see."
The ethereal being explained.
For some reason I believed them,
Though my terror felt barely contained.

"Do you see all these doors, different in ways?"
"Of course", I replied. "They're in all sizes and
shades."
"Each door has a key that unlocks to one of the
days
That you grew the most throughout your three
decades."

This revelation took some time to comprehend.
"Wait, they're time machines?" I gaped, aghast.
"In a sense, if you'd like to think of it like that."
"So I'm doomed to roam as a ghost from the
past?"

"No, of course not! Unless, that's what you
choose."
Then the friendly grim reaper beamed.
"Thank goodness", I sighed relieved, still
unconvinced this ordeal hadn't been dreamed.

"For the rest of eternity, you'll act as a guide
Watching over your soul, helping it to thrive.
Now, you'll speak to older versions of you
Who could use some advice on how to survive."

I blinked at the void, since they had no real face,
But before I could think, keys fell from the sky.
"They'll help you to make sense of your fate."
The figure whispered, "Go on, give them a try."

I picked up the keys, jangling loud.
And did my best to repress my overwhelm.
When I looked up, the cloaked one was gone.
It was time to enter my first new, old realm.

With shaking hands, I chose a key at whim.
I've been through worse, but not this surreal.
Then, I did what I always do to stop feeling.
I wrapped my heart up in comforting steel.

Apathy washed over my body, so freeing.
I was ready to see what the portal would reveal.
As long as I embraced this familiar numb,
I knew nothing could hurt me, no matter the
deal.

The key found its place inside,
So I turned it and the knob.
"Let's get this over with", I sighed.
But what I saw next made me instantly sob.

Little me looked up, clearly sad and alone,
Dressed in a yellow tutu, hair bun slicked back.
Her eyes looked too old for someone so young.
I know what they've seen. Every type of attack.

She threw herself at my legs, and there she
clung.
"She left me again", little me shook and cried.
"I thought I was being so good, this time!"
"She'll come for you soon, I promise", I lied.

"Someday you'll grow up and finally learn
That nobody loved you the way you deserved.
But it will be okay, you won't need anyone's
help.
You'll toughen your skin, so your heart is
preserved."

Then, I decided to never leave her again.
So I didn't.
That's it.

The end.